# MY FIRST PIANO

Ben Parker

## Learn To Play Right Away!

This Book Belongs To:

- - - - - - - - - - - - - - - - - - - - - - - -

Author: Ben Parker

Editor: Alison McNicol

First published in 2013 by Kyle Craig Publishing

This version updated Dec 2014



Design and illustration: Julie Anson

Music set by Ben Parker using Sibelius software

ISBN: 978 -1-908-707-17-8

A CIP record for this book is available from the British Library.

A Kyle Craig Publication
www.kyle-craig.com

# Contents


4 Welcome
Practice
5 Playing Position
6 Symbols In Music
8 Let's Get Playing – Middle C
10 New Note D In The Right Hand
11 Playing With Your Left Hand
12 New Note B In The Left Hand
13 Note Lengths
15 New Note E In The Right Hand
3/4 or Waltz Time
16 New Note A In The Left Hand
17 New Note F In The Right Hand
New Note G In The Left Hand
19 Rests
23 Moving Between Hands
25 Changing Hand Positions
27 Using Both Hands At The Same Time
31 Eighth Notes
34 The Other Notes
36 Quiz!
38 Left Hand Notes
39 Right Hand Notes

# INTRODUCTION

## Welcome to My First Piano book!

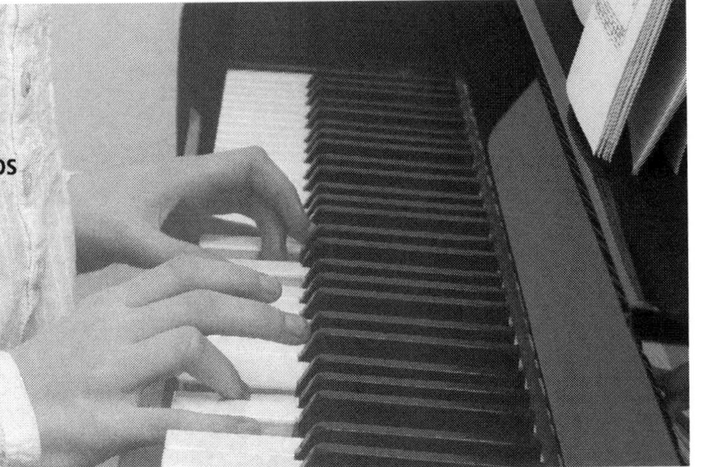

The piano is one of the most popular musical instruments to learn, and you will have tons of fun learning to play! Simply follow the steps in this book, practice regularly, and you will soon be playing your first tunes in no time!

Also included in this book is a step by step guide to reading music.

### Practice: Note To Parents

Like any skill, playing an instrument takes a lot of practice. Practicing more regularly for shorter lengths of time is more effective than practicing for an hour or so just once a week.

The minimum amount would be around 15-20 minutes 3 to 4 times a week. The ideal amount would be 20 minutes a day, 7 days a week. Maybe set out a plan of your week and work out the best times to fit your practicing around the other things you do. The more your practice can become part of your weekly or daily routine the better.

It is the returning to the instrument that will make your practice time more worthwhile. So remember little and often is better than a lot, less often.

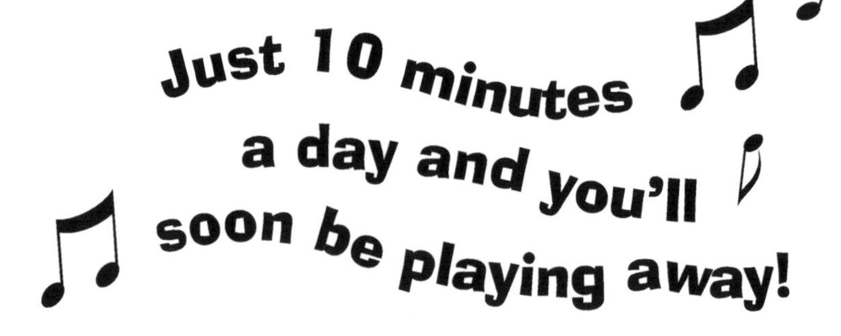

# Playing Position

You should always try to sit with your back straight on a suitable stool/chair. Your forearms should be at the same level as the keyboard. Your hands should never reach up to the keys. You may have to experiment with the height of your seat.

## Hand Position

Your hands should be moved from the wrist. You should keep your wrists in line with your hands. Your fingers should be slightly bent and should adopt a 'half claw' position on the keys.

## Your Fingers

The fingers of both your hands are numbered to help us know which fingers should play which notes. The thumb is number 1 on each hand:

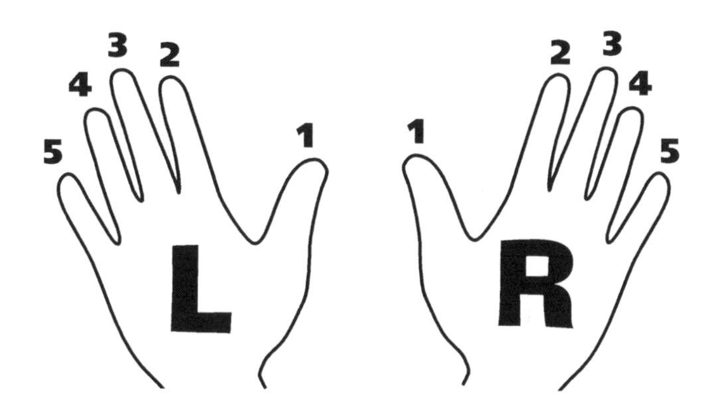

# Symbols in Music

## The Clefs

There are two staves in all piano music. These are made up of 5 lines each. The top stave is for the **RIGHT HAND** and uses the **treble clef** at the beginning:

The bottom stave is for the **LEFT HAND** and uses the **bass clef** at the beginning:

## Time Signatures

Music is divided up into **bars**. Bars have a certain number of **beats**. The **time signature** is two numbers sat on top of each other at the beginning of every piece of music — the TOP number tells us how many beats there are in each bar:

$\frac{4}{4}$ A time signature showing **FOUR** beats in each bar

$\frac{3}{4}$ A time signature showing **THREE** beats in each bar

$\frac{2}{4}$ A time signature showing **TWO** beats in each bar

Here's how it looks on the staves:

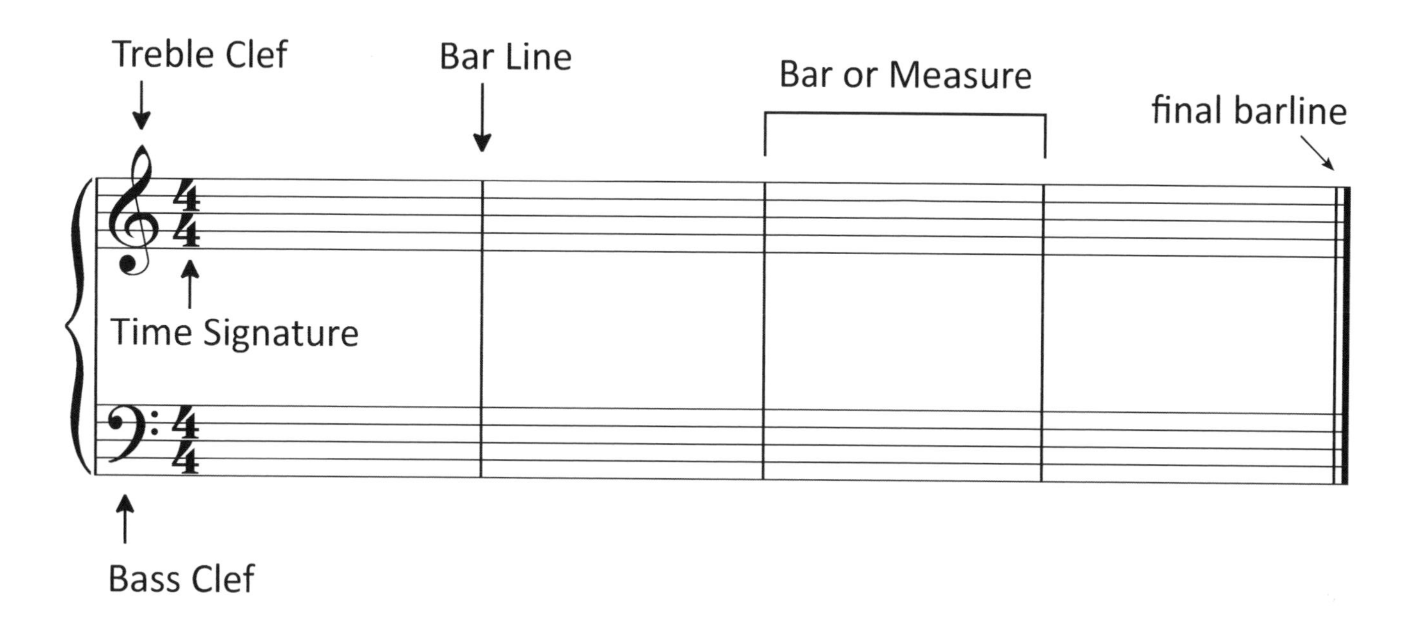


## The Keyboard

Although you may recognize it instantly, the piano keyboard may be confusing for a beginner. It is made up of white and black keys — the black keys are grouped in pairs and in threes.

This regular pattern of black notes is repeated all the way along the keyboard and it helps us to work out where all the notes are. Almost like a map.

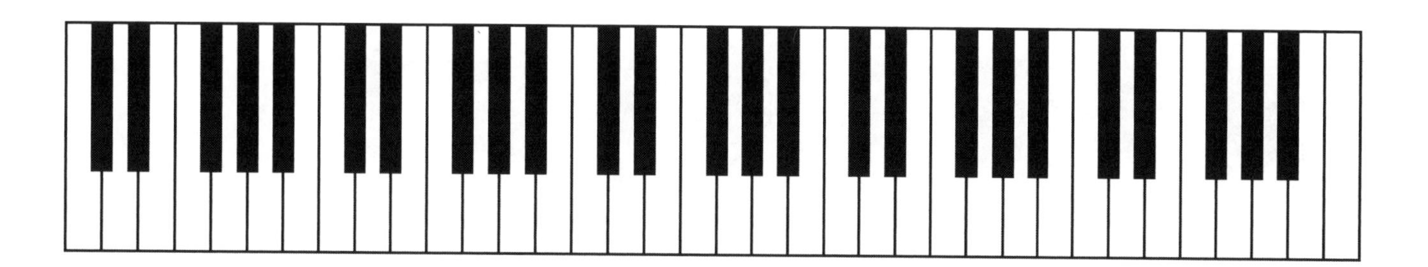

# Let's Get Playing – The Middle C

To get us started, let's find the note **Middle C**. This is the white note to the left of the pair of black notes on your piano (often nearest to the lock for the piano lid).

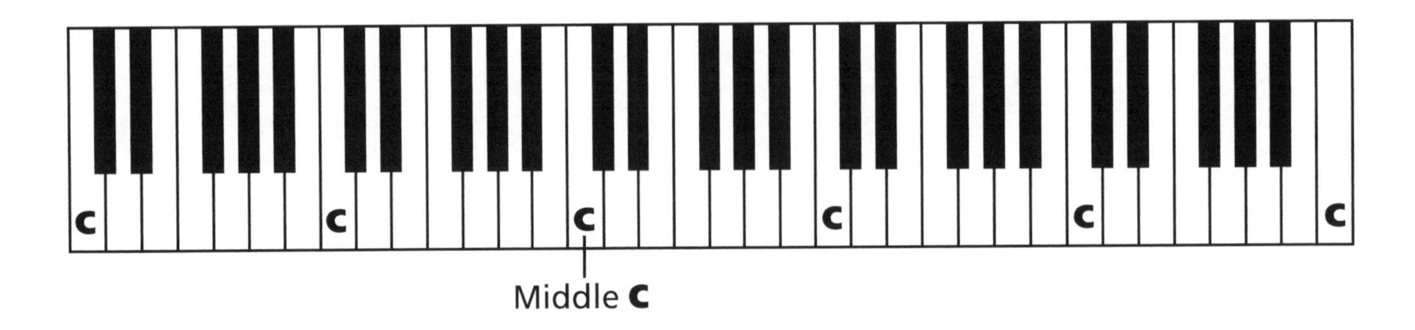


First of all let's see what the **Middle C** looks like in music — notice the small number 1 below it — this is there to remind us to play the **Middle C** with finger 1 (the thumb) of the right hand.

The note shown is a **WHOLE NOTE**. You count this for **FOUR** beats.

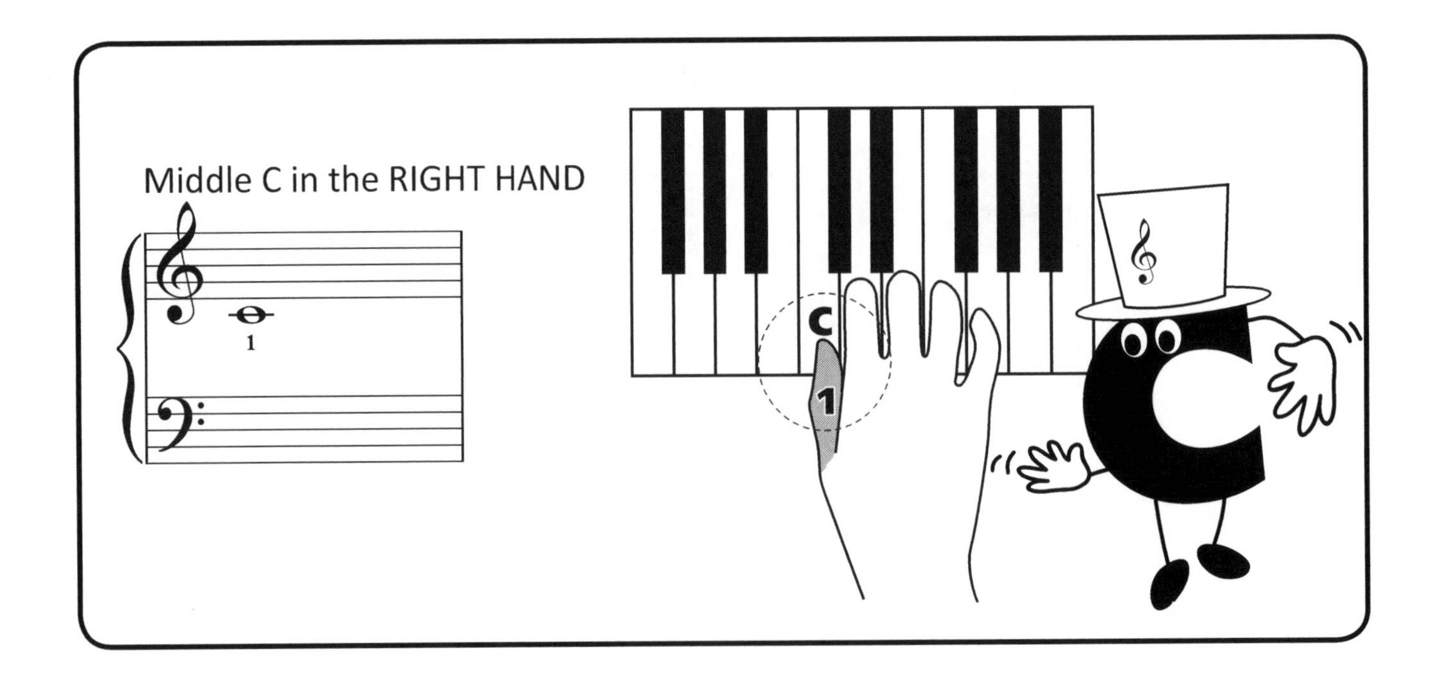

Try playing two whole note **middle C's** in a row. **Count 1** as your thumb pushes down on the key then **count to 4** before you play your next **C**:

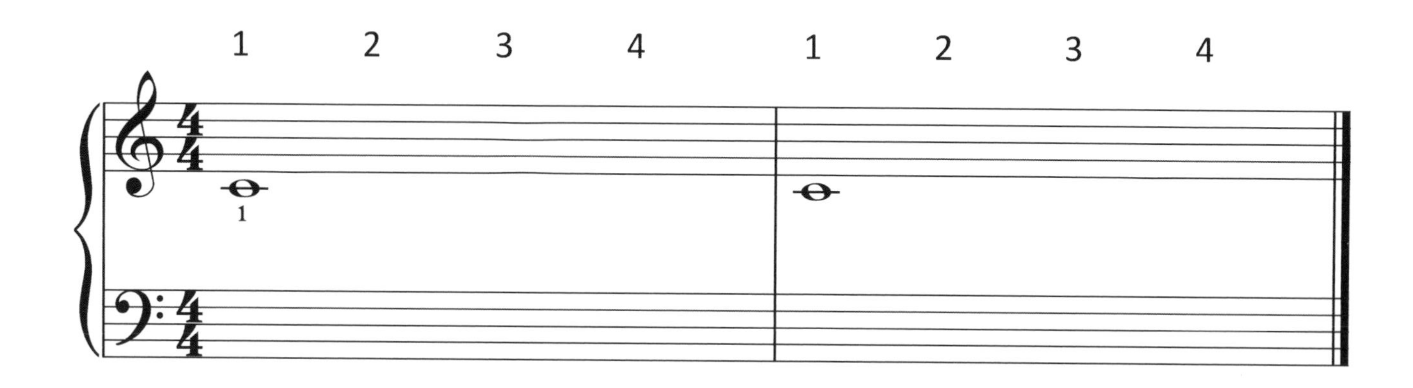


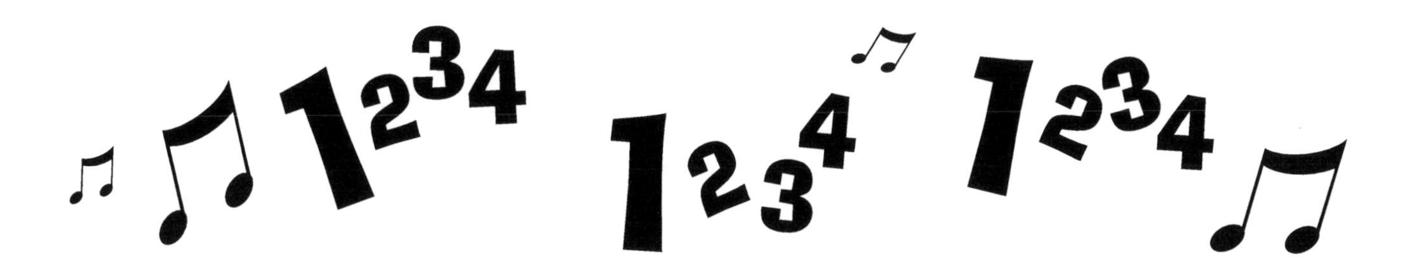


Now lets try using the same note but with **quarter notes**. These last for 1 beat each so there are 4 of them in each bar:

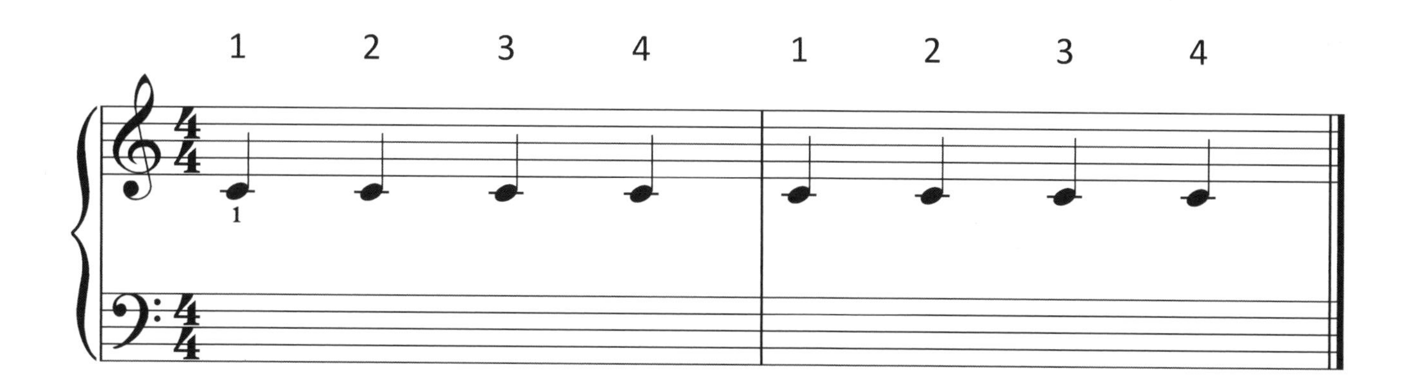

# Playing With Your Left Hand

Now let's try playing with our left hand.

In the left hand, the **middle C** is also played with finger number 1 (the thumb). The left hand stave is written using a **bass clef**.

Counting 4 beats in each bar try your left hand **C** as quarter notes:

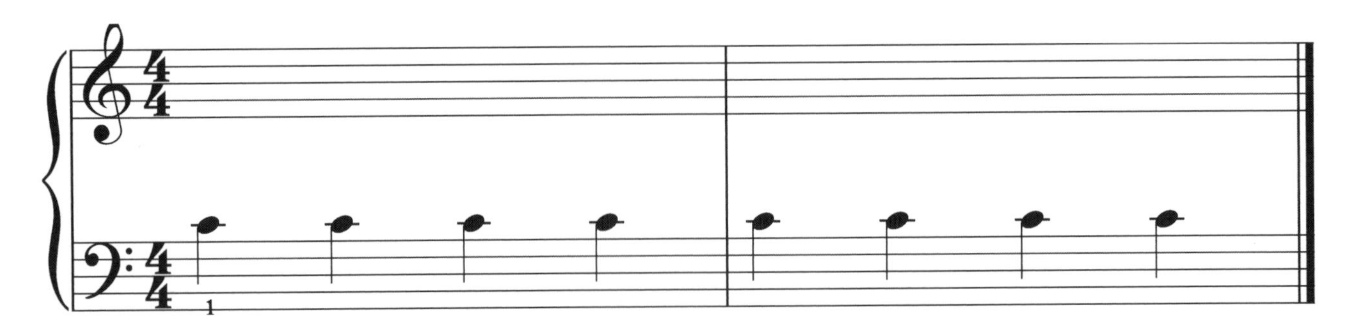

# New Note D In The Right Hand

Now let's try a new note!

Your new note **D** is played with the second finger of your right hand:

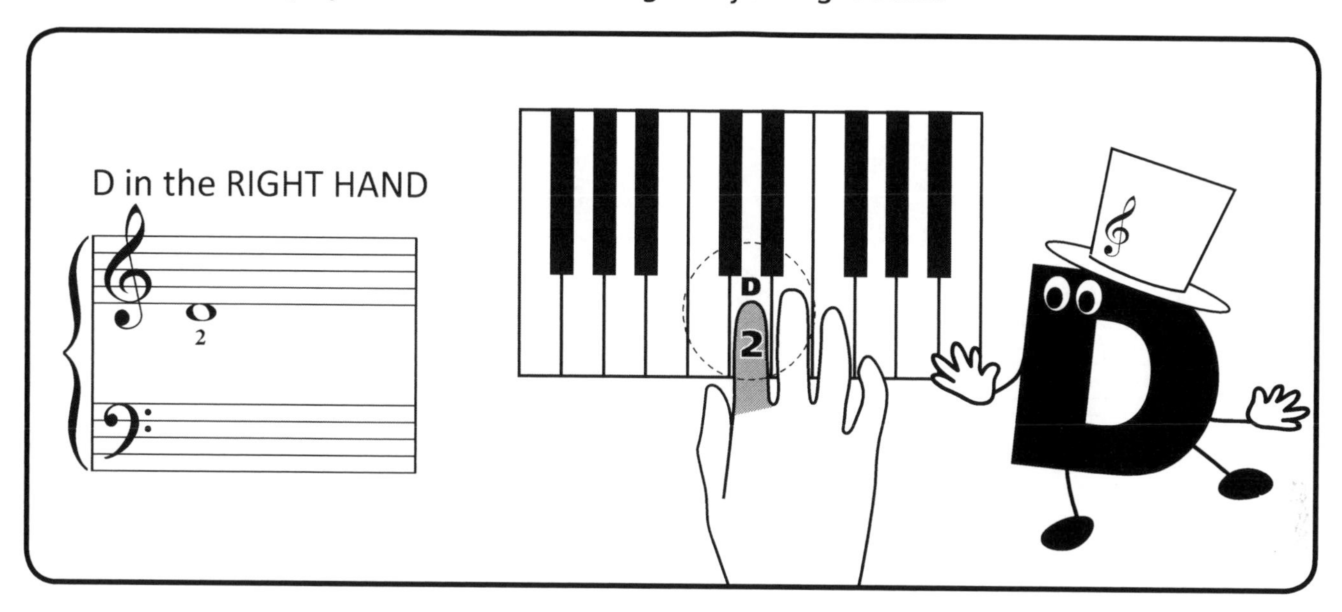


## One Step Up

# New Note B In The Left Hand

Your new note **B** is played with the second finger of your left hand:

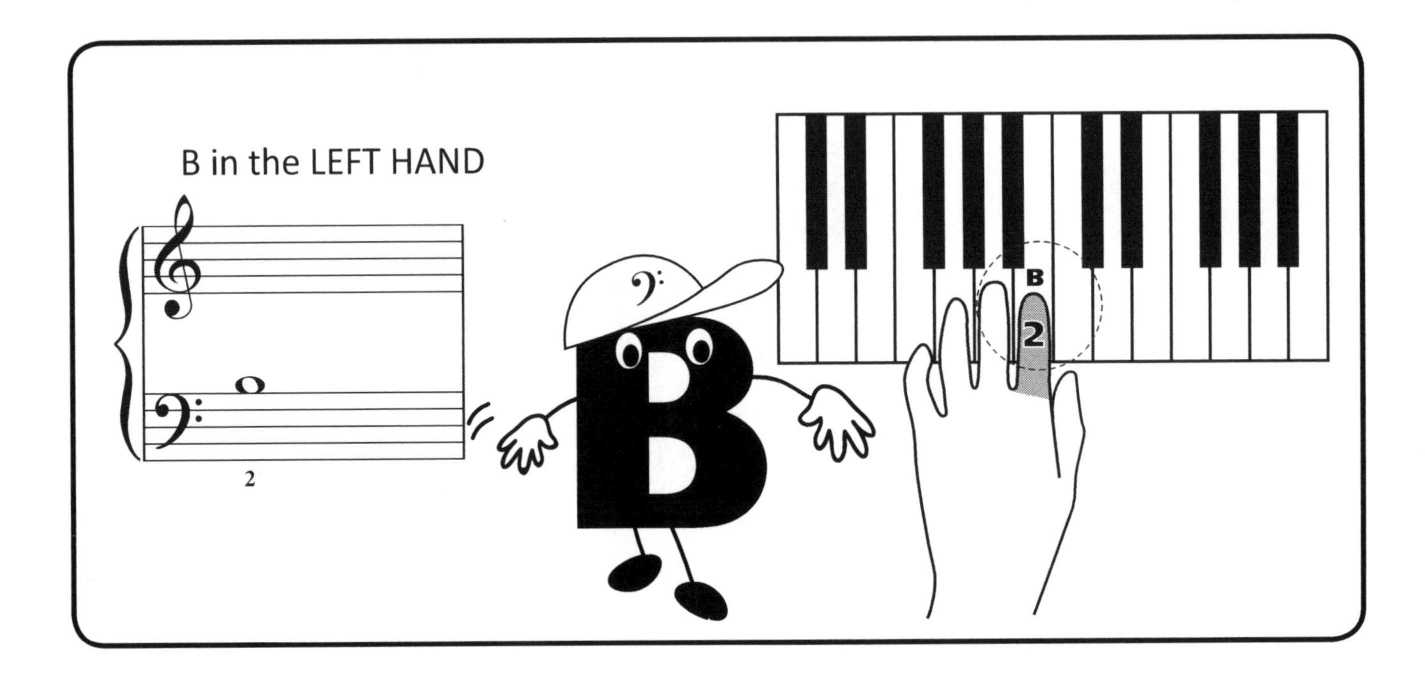


## Get Down

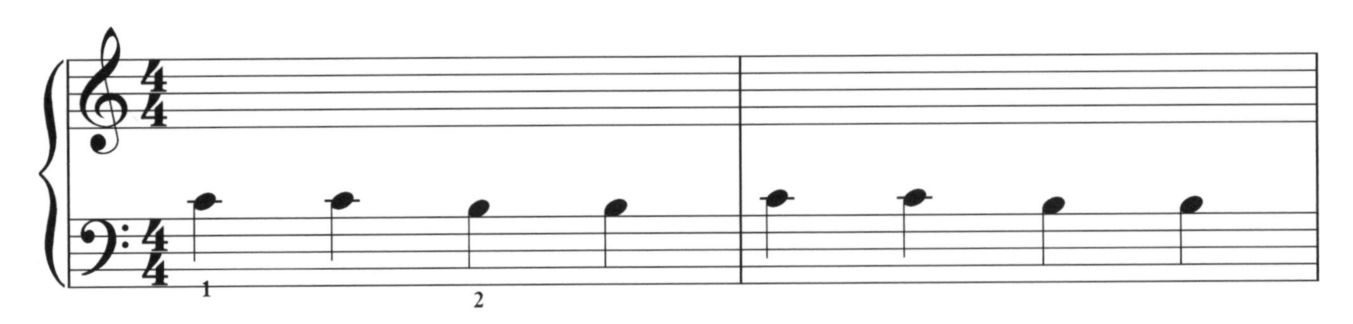

# Note Lengths

So far we have looked at **whole notes** (four beats) and **quarter notes** (1 beat).

Let's see the two other types of notes we'll use in this book — the **half note** (2 beats) and the **eighth note** (half a beat).

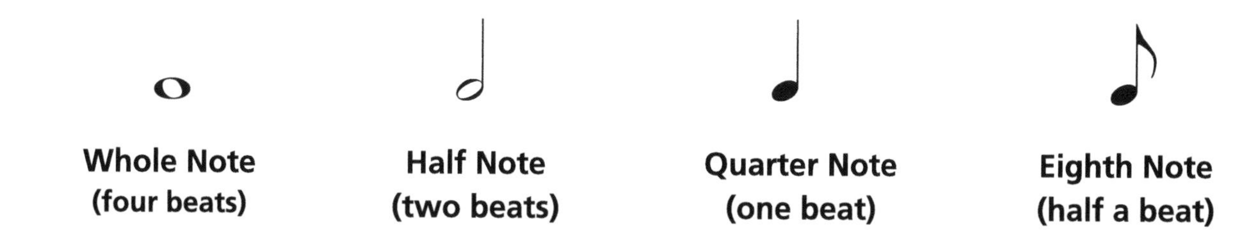


The next piece has both quarter notes and half notes in BOTH hands! Make sure you count carefully as you play — the main beat count is written above the treble clef to help you see where the notes are in the bar.

## Two Hands Luke

**'Long Road Home'** has all your longer notes in. The whole note lasting for four beats and the half note lasting for two. Count carefully through this and be patient with those long notes!

## Long Road Home

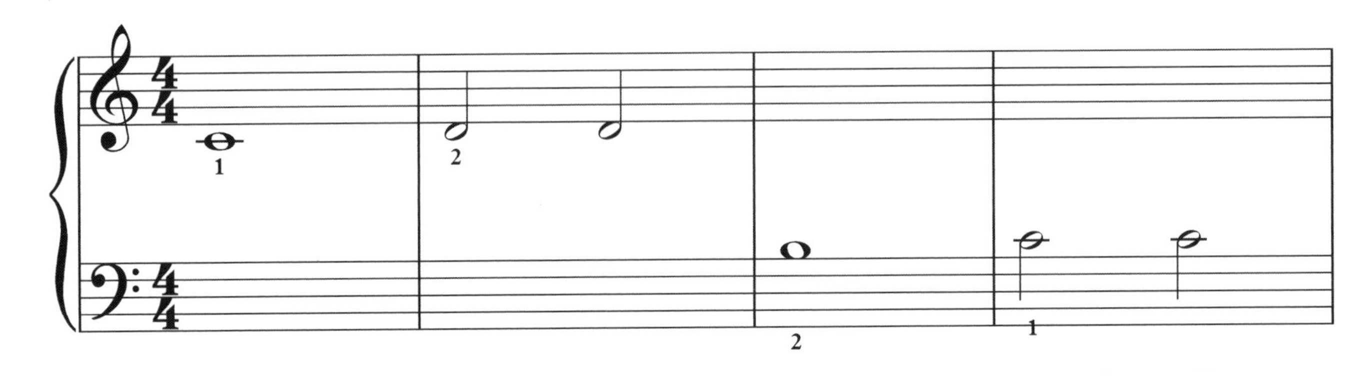

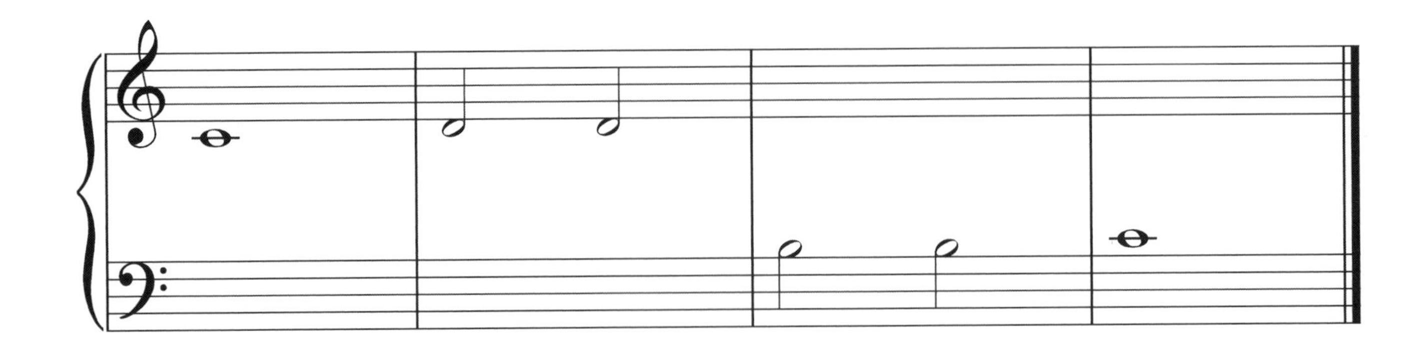

# New Note E in the Right Hand

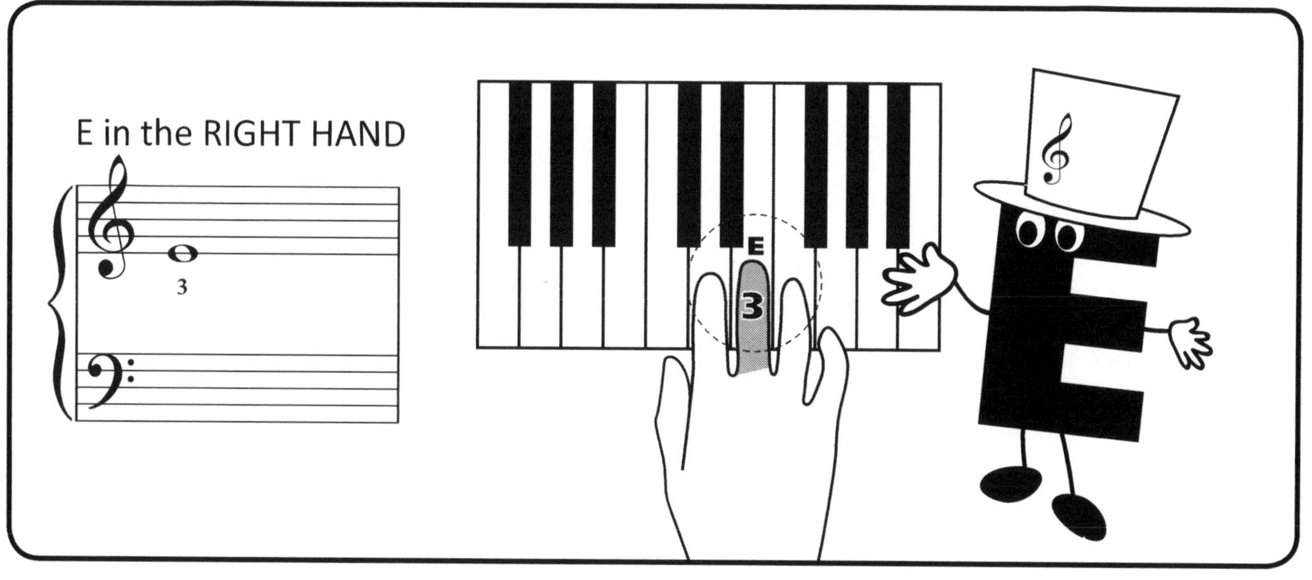


# 3/4 or Waltz Time

So far all of our music has been written with 4 beats to a bar. 4/4 is probably the most common time signature you will come across. Another time signature you will see a lot is 3/4 (three beats in a bar). Commonly known as **Waltz time** it was also a popular dance in the late 18th century.

The important thing to remember when counting and playing 3/4 time is to think of beat 1 as a STRONG beat whilst beats 2 & 3 are weaker. In the exercise below the counts are written above the music with beat 1 in **BOLD** to help show the stronger beat. Try playing the note on the first beat a little bit louder than the following 2. The last note is a dotted half note — you play this for 3 beats.

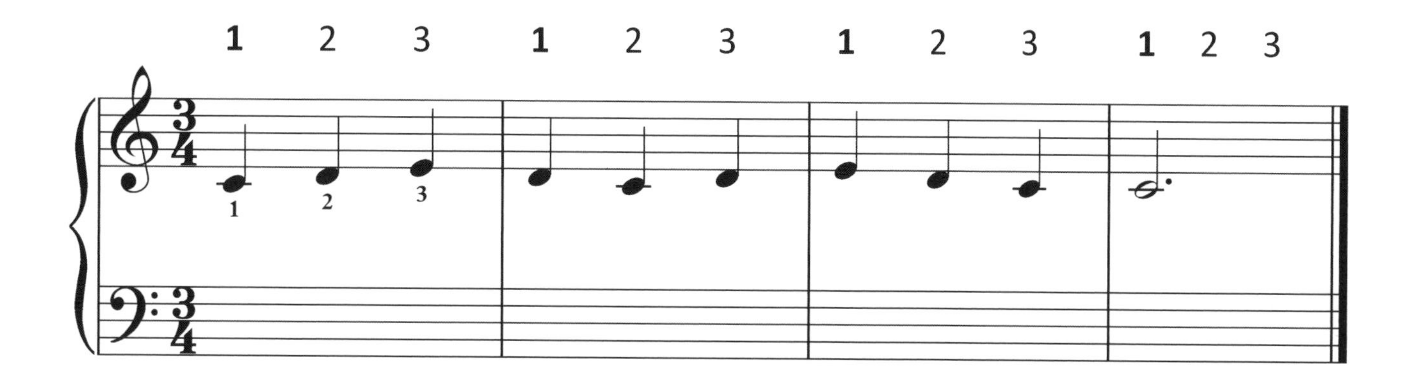

# New Note A In The Left Hand

## Dancing Shoes

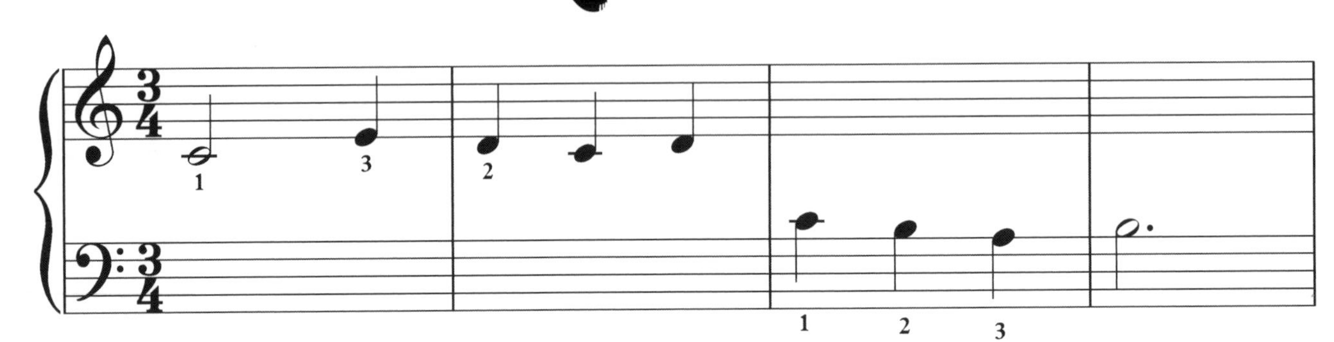

# New Note F In The Right Hand

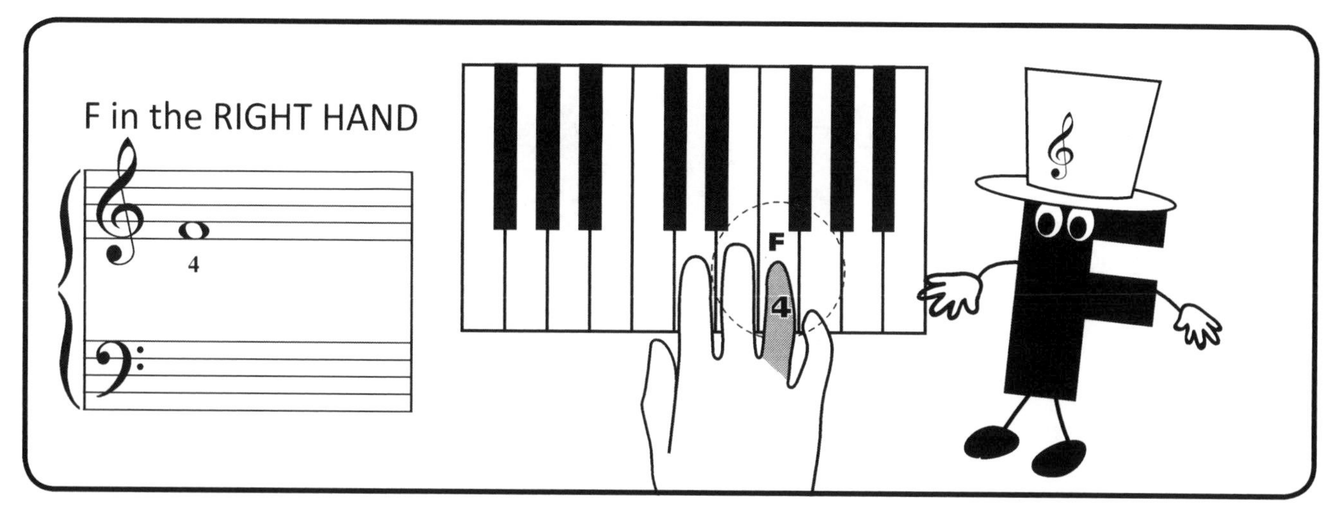

# New Note G In The Left Hand

Try this short piece. It will help you get used to your new notes

## Upstairs And Downstairs

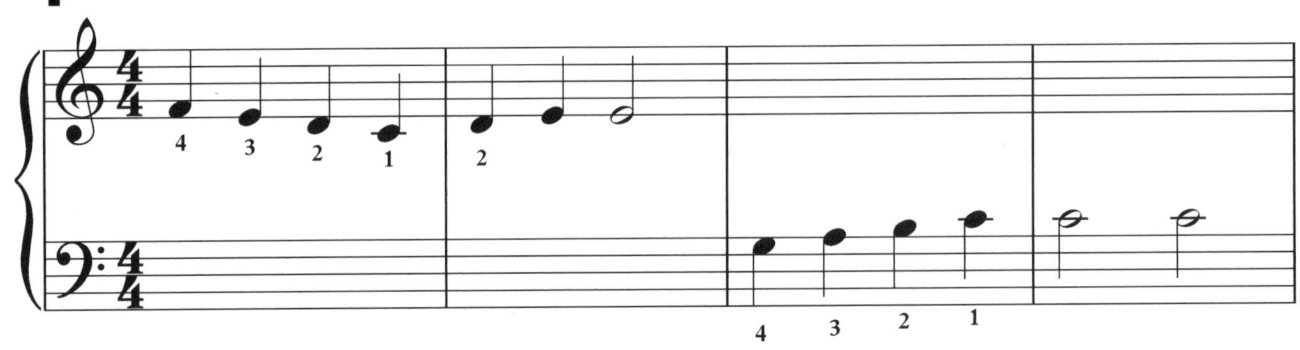

# Rests

Rests tell us when not to play. Like notes, they last for different lengths of time. These different lengths are shown as different symbols:

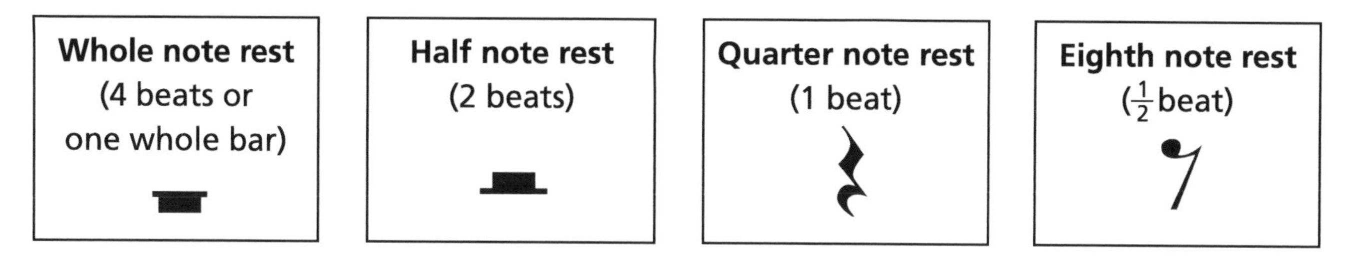


Try **'Rest Up'** — it has whole, half and quarter note rests so make sure you count through the bars carefully.

The well-known tune for **'Mary Had A Little Lamb'** is played here in the right hand only. Whole bar rests are used to tell us to rest the left hand throughout. It also has your new note **G** in the right hand.

## Mary Had A Little Lamb

# Twinkle Twinkle

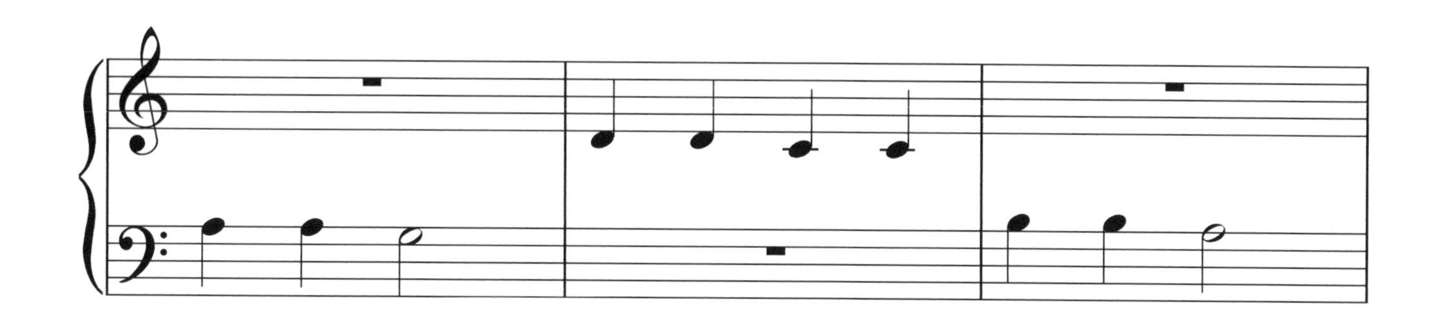

## Stop The Beat

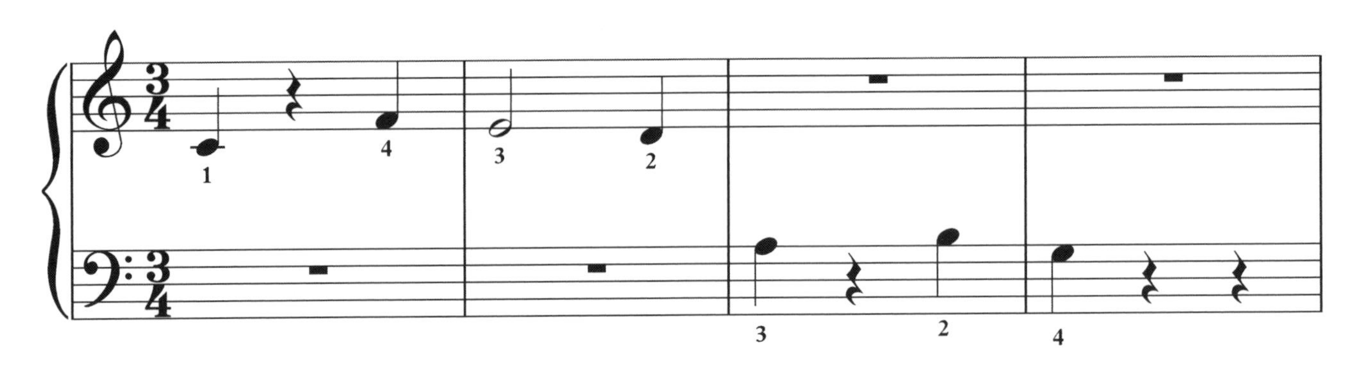

# Moving Between Hands

In **'London Bridge Is Falling Down'** there is more movement between the hands. Make sure you keep the fingers of each hand over the top of the notes they play.

## London Bridge Is Falling Down

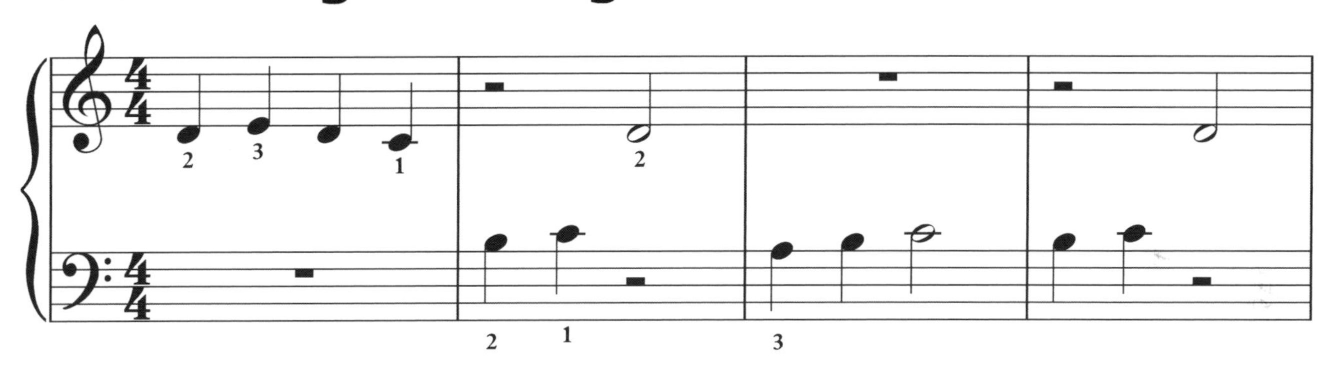

## Yankee Doodle

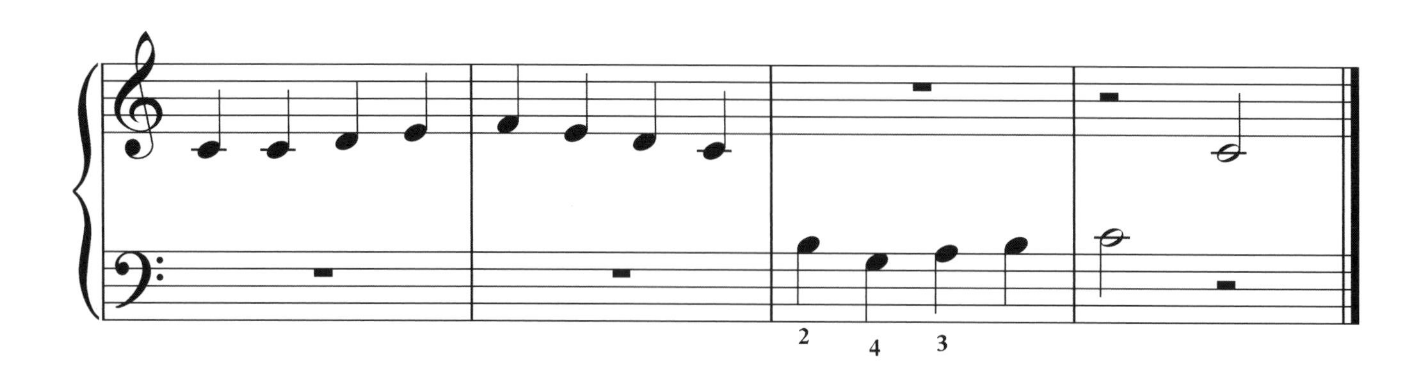

# Changing Hand Positions

So far we have stuck closely to having the thumbs of each hand covering the **middle C** note. Now let's try moving the left hand position so the left hand thumb now plays the **lower G** note.

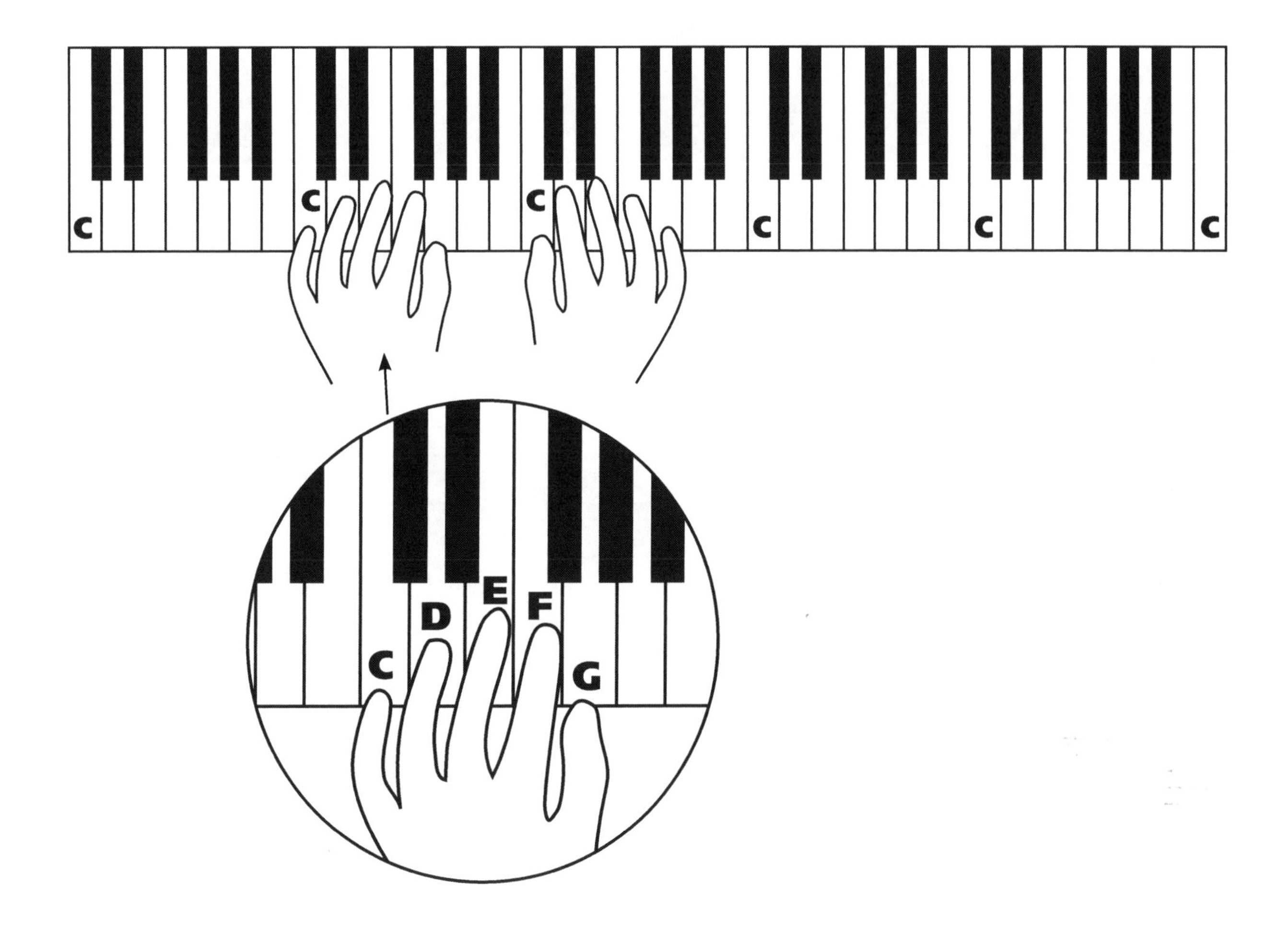


How this looks on the left hand (**bass clef**) stave with the little finger (number 5) playing the **C** below.

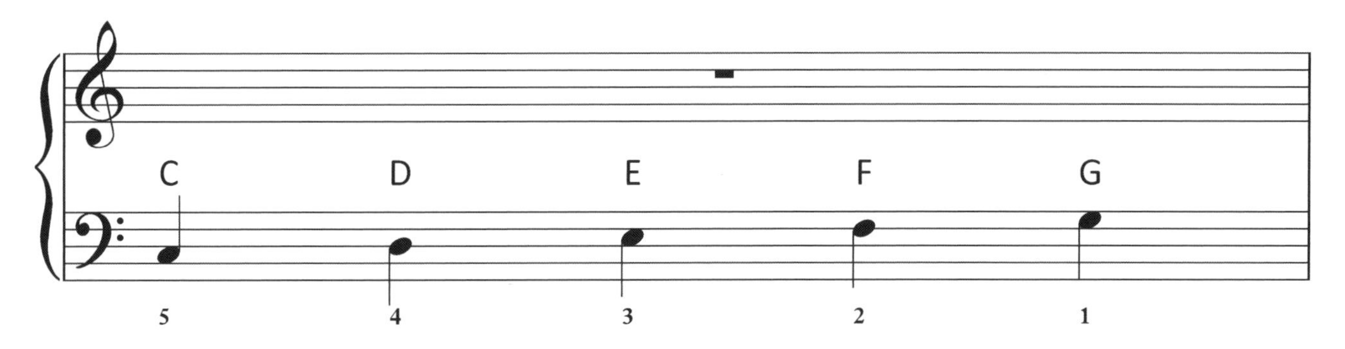

At the end of line two of 'Row, Row' you'll see a **tie** (curved line) between two notes. This joins them together (two dotted half notes tied = 6 beats)

## Row, Row, Row Your Boat

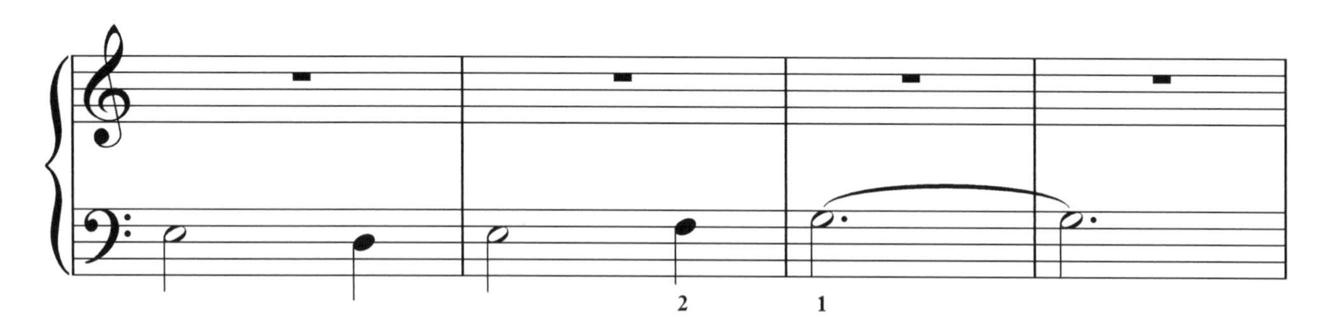


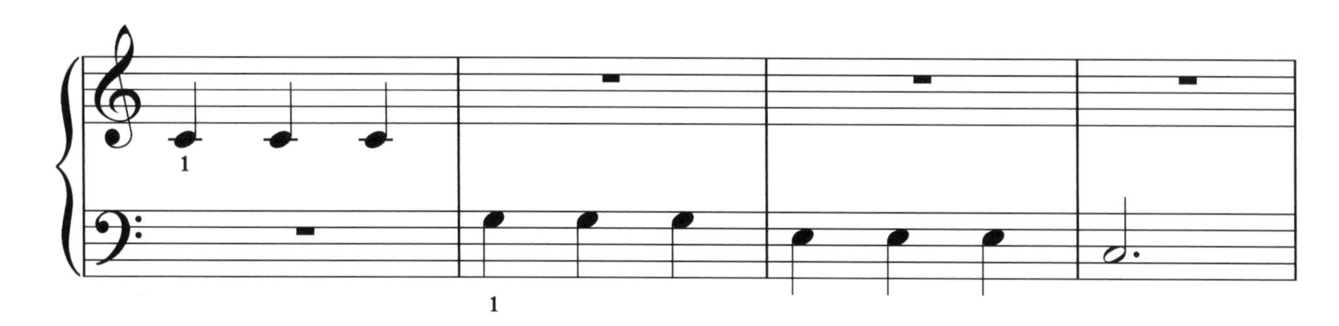


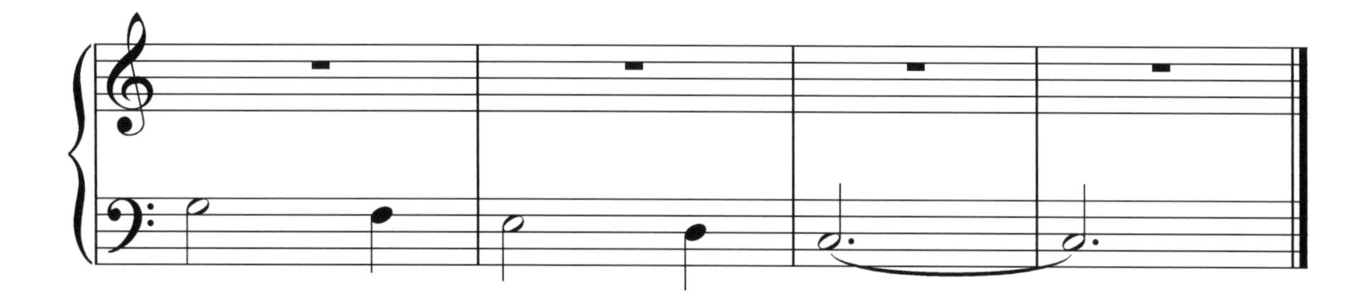

# Using Both Hands At The Same Time

Now let's try a very simple exercise to get you used playing with both hands at the same time. Remember your fingering for your left hand notes. Make sure you start with your left hand little finger (finger 5) on the **C** below **middle C**.

Now let's add some movement to your left hand part, keeping the right hand the same:

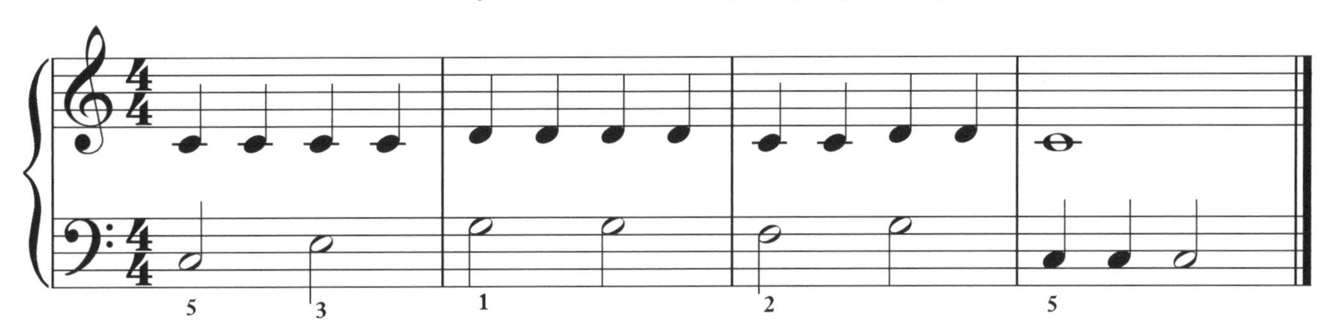

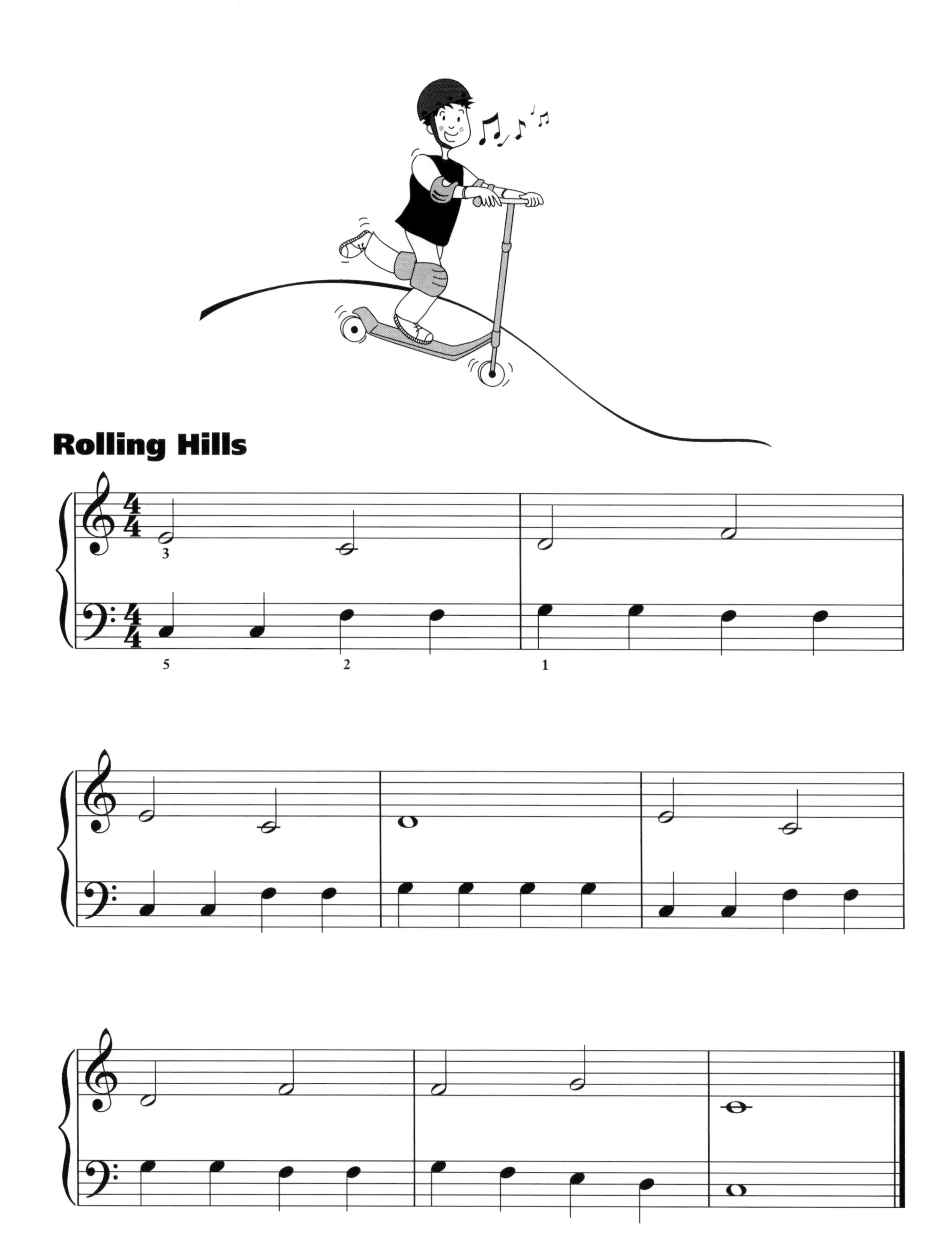
Rolling Hills
3
5
2
1

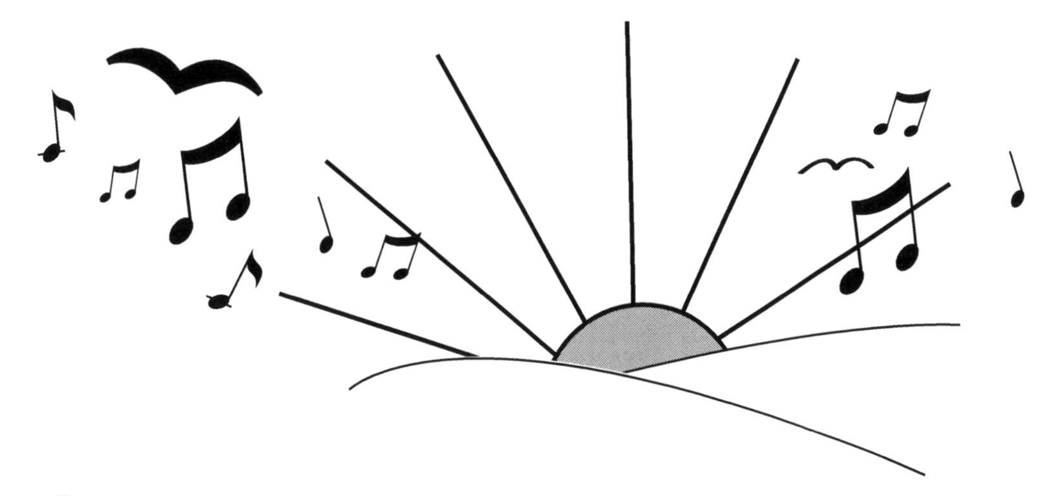

## Sunrise

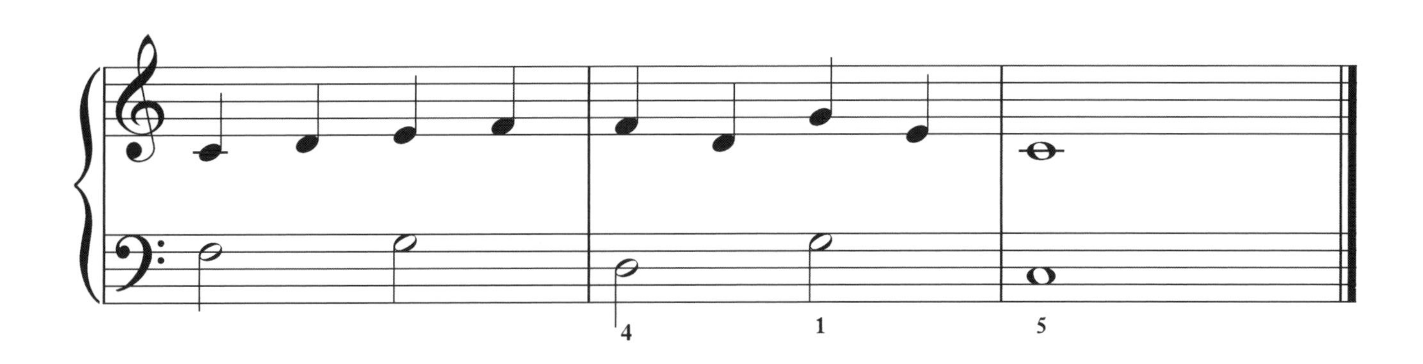

# Slow Dance

# Eighth Notes

So far we've only used whole notes, half notes and quarter notes. Our new note length is an **eighth** note. This is also known as a **quaver**. These last for half a beat. When counting eighth notes use 1 & 2 & 3 & 4 &. This will help you with the rhythm.

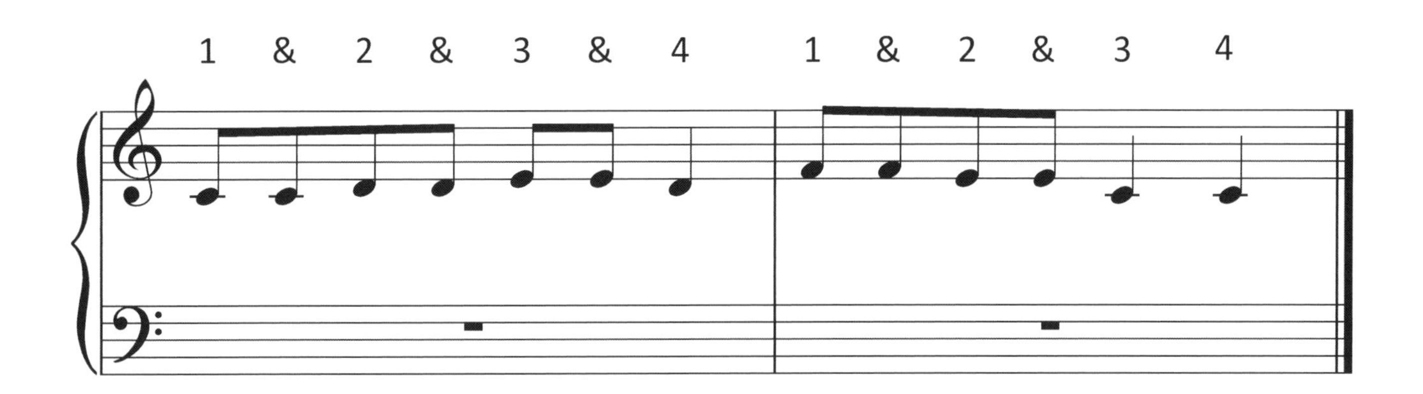

## Oranges And Lemons

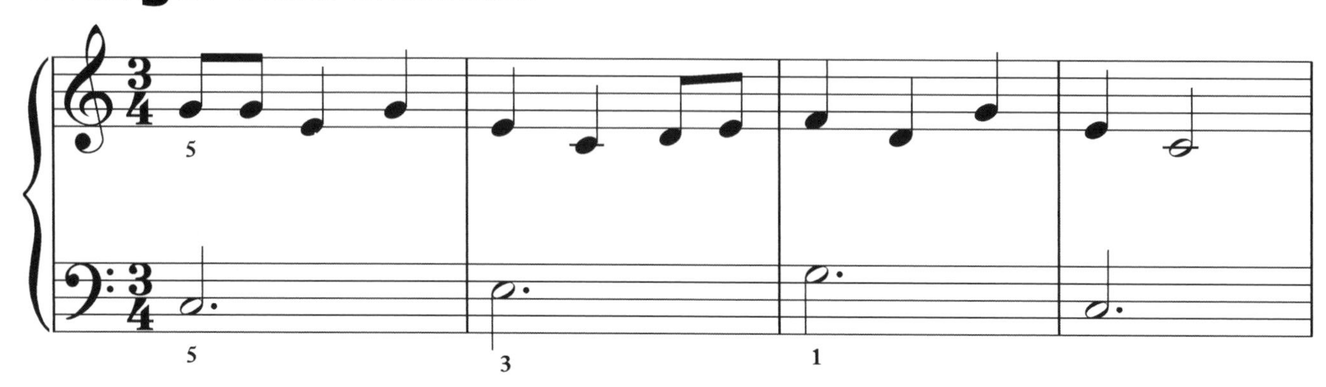

# Jingle Bells

# The Other Notes

There are other notes on your treble and bass clef staves as well as the notes you can play with each of the five fingers of your two hands. As your playing develops you'll need these notes to play more difficult pieces.

Notice that the notes are on the lines or in the spaces between them. To help us remember these other notes we have some handy fun phrases:

## The Notes on the Right Hand Stave (Treble Clef)

### Notes in the spaces

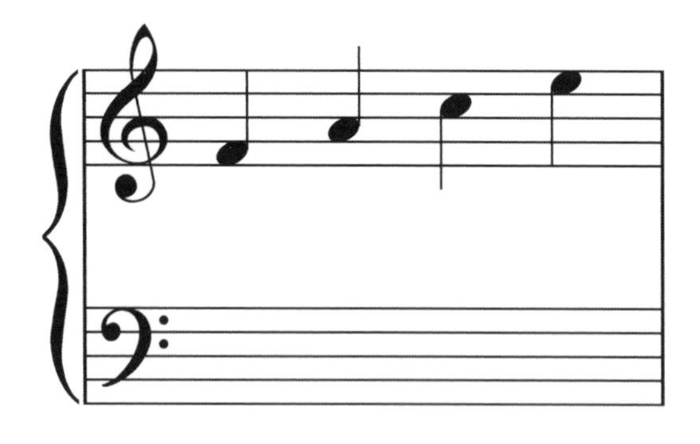

**F A C E**

### Notes on the lines

**E G B D F**

# The Notes On The Left Hand Stave (Bass Clef)

**Notes on the lines**

**G B D F A**

**Notes in the spaces**

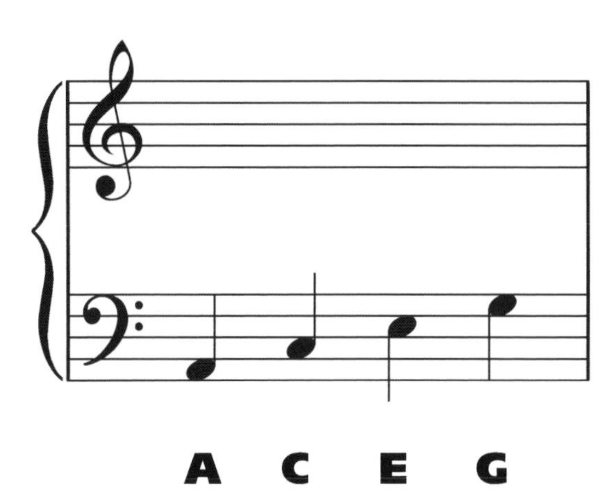

**A C E G**

# Quiz!

## NAME THAT NOTE!

## How many beats do each of these notes last for?

HALF/ONE/TWO/FOUR HALF/ONE/TWO/FOUR HALF/ONE/TWO/FOUR HALF/ONE/TWO/FOUR

# Quiz!

**Can you fill in the correct RIGHT HAND NOTE names on the keys below?**

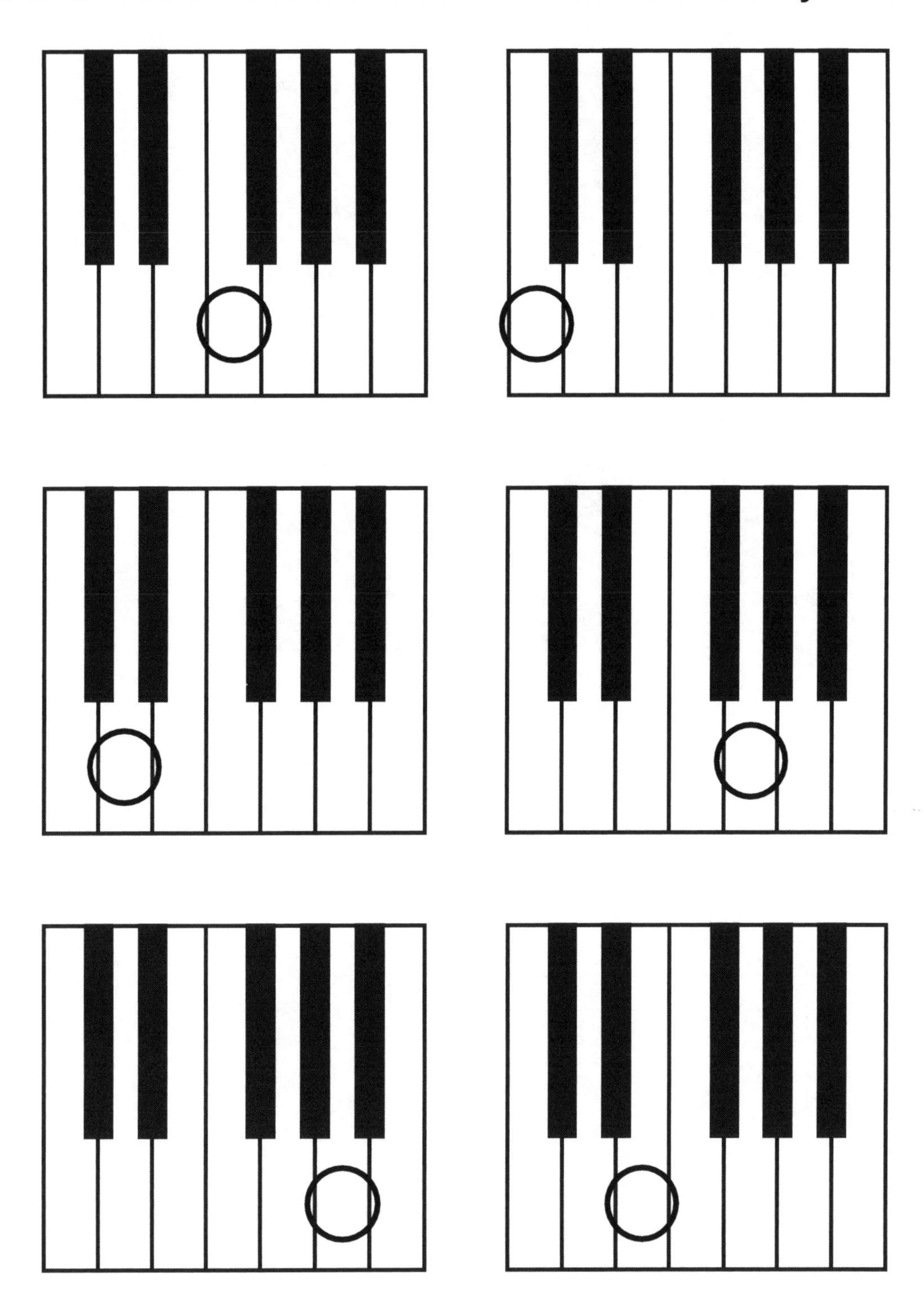

# Right Hand Notes

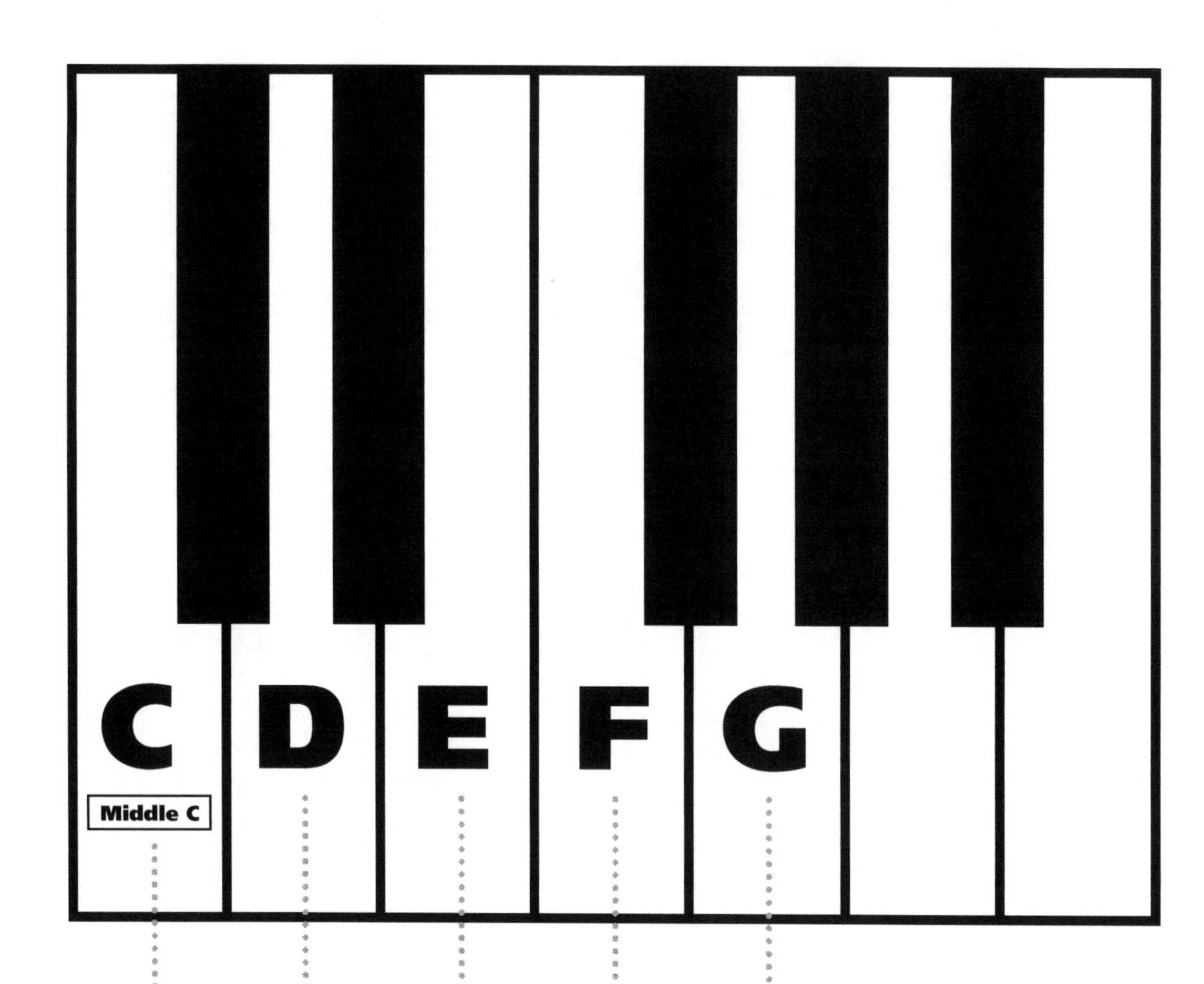


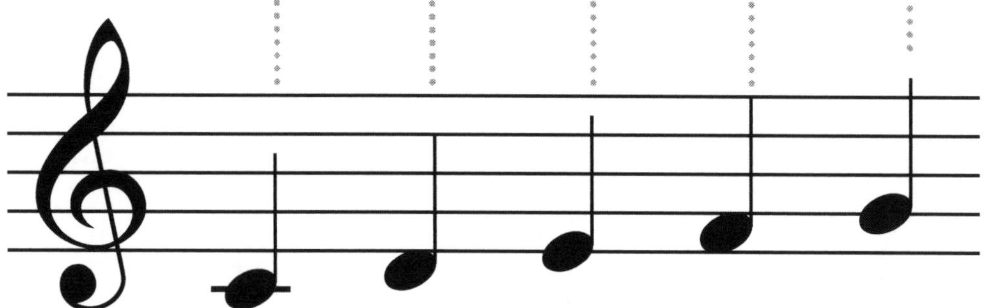

# Left Hand Notes

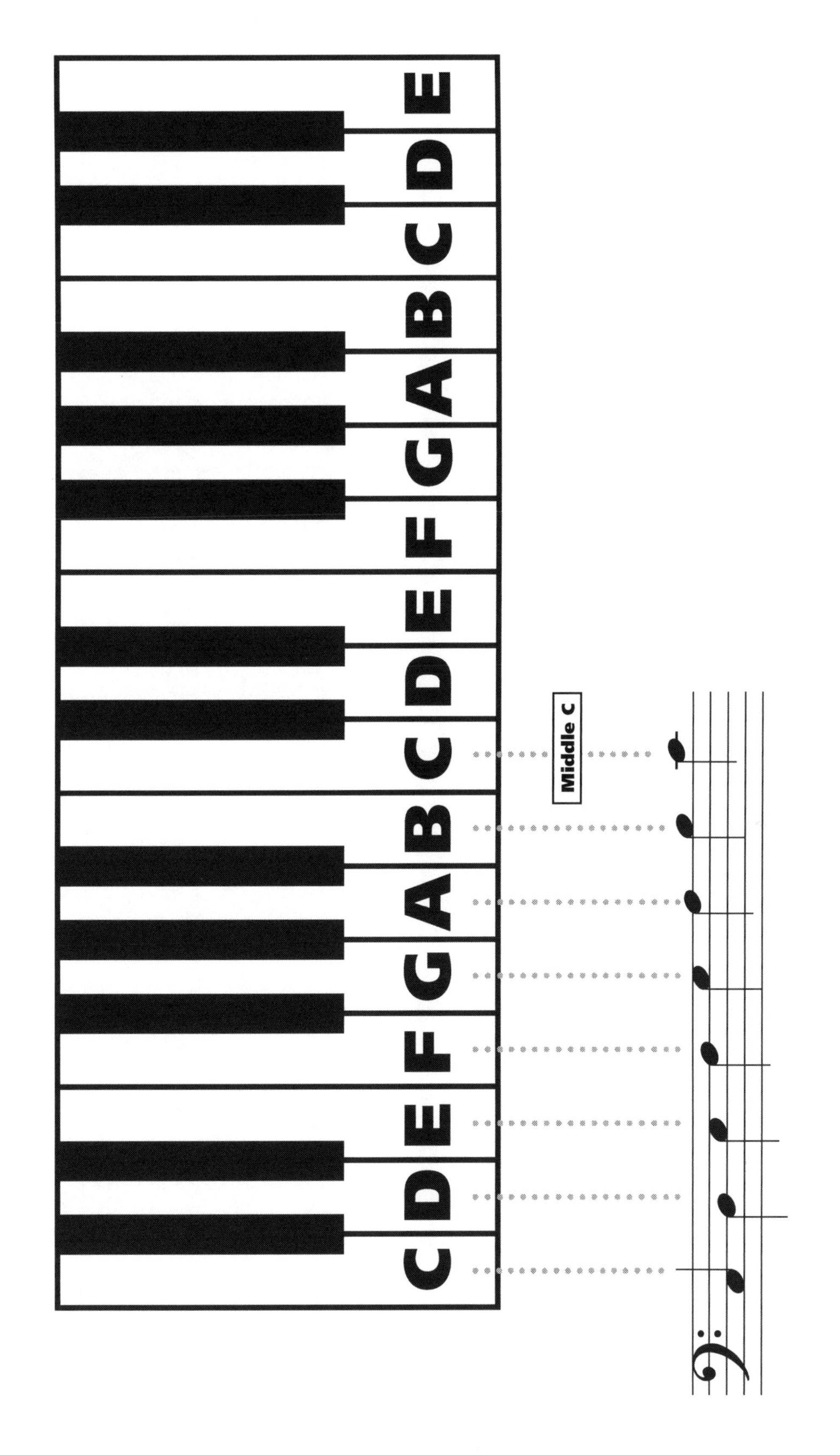

# MORE GREAT MUSIC BOOKS FROM KYLE CRAIG!

**How To Play UKULELE —** A Complete Guide for Absolute Beginners

**978-1-908-707-08-6**

**My First UKULELE —** Learn to Play: Kids

**978-1-908-707-11-6**

**Easy UKULELE Tunes**

**978-1-908707-37-6**

**How To Play GUITAR —** A Complete Guide for Absolute Beginners

**978-1-908-707-09-3**

**My First GUITAR —** Learn to Play: Kids

**978-1-908-707-13-0**

**Easy GUITAR Tunes**

**978-1-908707-34-5**

**How To Play KEYBOARD —** A Complete Guide for Absolute Beginners

**978-1-908-707-14-7**

**My First KEYBOARD —** Learn to Play: Kids

**978-1-908-707-15-4**

**Easy KEYBOARD Tunes**

**978-1-908707-35-2**

**How To Play PIANO —** A Complete Guide for Absolute Beginners

**978-1-908-707-16-1**

**My First PIANO —** Learn to Play: Kids

**978-1-908-707-17-8**

**Easy PIANO Tunes**

**978-1-908707-33-8**

**How To Play HARMONICA —** A Complete Guide for Absolute Beginners

**978-1-908-707-28-4**

**My First RECORDER —** Learn to Play: Kids

**978-1-908-707-18-5**

**Easy RECORDER Tunes**

**978-1-908707-36-9**

**How To Play BANJO —** A Complete Guide for Absolute Beginners

**978-1-908-707-19-2**

**The GUITAR Chord Dictionary**

**978-1-908707-39-0**

**The UKULELE Chord Dictionary**

**978-1-908707-38-3**